MILITARY SPECIAL OPS

ARMY
SPECIAL FORCES

ELITE OPERATIONS

BY PATRICIA NEWMAN

Lerner Publications Company
Minneapolis

Lerner Publications Company
A division of Lerner Publishing Group, Inc.
241 First Avenue North
Minneapolis, MN 55401 U.S.A.

Website address: www.lernerbooks.com

Content Consultant: Kalev Sepp, assistant professor, Naval Postgraduate School

Library of Congress Cataloging-in-Publication Data

Newman, Patricia, 1958-
    Army Special Forces : elite operations / by Patricia Newman.
        pages cm. — (Military special ops)
    Includes index.
    ISBN 978-0-7613-9076-3 (lib. bdg. : alk. paper)
    ISBN 978-1-4677-1764-9 (eBook)
    1. United States. Army. Special Forces—Juvenile literature. I. Title.
UA34.S64N498 2014
356'.160973—dc23   2012048176

Manufactured in the United States of America
1 — MG — 7/15/13

The images in this book are used with the permission of: © Aleksandar Mijatovic/Shutterstock Images, backgrounds; U.S. Department of Defense, 5, 7, 11, 12–13, 16, 28; © Rafiq Maqbool/AP Images, 6; Library of Congress, 9; Russell Lee Klika/U.S. Army, 15; © John McConnico/AP Images, 17; U.S. Army, 19; 1st Special Forces Group (Airborne)/U.S. Army Special Operations Command, 20; U.S. National Guard, 21; © U.S. Army/ AP Images, 22; © Nancy Nehring/iStockphoto, 23; Tony R. Ritter/U.S. Air Force, 24, 26; Gonzalo J. Gonzalez/U.S. Army, 25; U.S. Army John F. Kennedy Special Warfare Center and School, 27; Matthew Bruch/U.S. Air Force, 29.

Front cover: U.S. Air Force photo by Tech. Sgt. DeNoris Mickle.

Main body text set in Tw Cen MT Std Medium 12/18.
Typeface provided by Adobe Systems.

CONTENTS

CHAPTER ONE
TO FREE THE OPPRESSED 4

CHAPTER TWO
THE GROWTH OF ARMY SPECIAL FORCES 8

CHAPTER THREE
WARRIOR DIPLOMATS 14

CHAPTER FOUR
THE SPECIAL FORCES' BAG OF TRICKS 18

CHAPTER FIVE
THE PATH TO THE GREEN BERET 24

GLOSSARY 30

LEARN MORE 31

INDEX 32

ABOUT THE AUTHOR 32

CHAPTER ONE:
TO FREE THE OPPRESSED

The mission began on a cold night in November 2001. High winds buffeted the heavy helicopter. Thirteen U.S. Army Special Forces soldiers crouched in the freezing chopper. They finally landed on a snow-covered mountain in Afghanistan. The men carried 100-pound (45 kilogram) packs. A campfire in the distance lighted their way. Operation Enduring Freedom had begun.

They reached the campfire and met their Afghan guides. Together, the group walked many long, cold miles. They were going to meet one of the Afghan Northern Alliance commanders. Their mission: break the Taliban's hold over Afghanistan.

THE TALIBAN

The Soviet Union (a union of fifteen republics that included Russia) occupied Afghanistan from 1979 to 1989. Many Afghans fought to free their country. When the Soviets finally withdrew, the Taliban seized power. The Taliban made strict rules to impose their idea of order. Kite flying, music, television, and the Internet were outlawed. Girls were not allowed to attend school. Women could no longer work outside the home as they had for most of the twentieth century. Men had to wear beards. Punishments included beatings, cutting off fingers, and death by shooting.

Army Special Forces have played a crucial role in the conflict in Afghanistan.

For two days, the Special Forces team walked without sleep. They picked their way down icy trails and across steep cliffs. They needed the Afghan commander's help to drive the Taliban out of an important city. First, the Special Forces had to win his trust. When the sun rose on the third day, the soldiers reached a tiny village. The Afghan commander came out of a mud hut. The former schoolteacher wore a long beard. He greeted them in his native language, Dari.

None of the Special Forces soldiers spoke Dari, but Special Forces members are trained to work around these types of problems. The team members tried English, Chinese, Arabic, and French. The Afghan commander did not understand them. Finally, one man tried Russian. That worked!

The Afghan commander's army was poorly equipped and hungry. The Special Forces team called for cargo planes. They parachuted in food, clothing, and ammunition. Bringing these supplies built trust between the Americans and the Afghans.

The Special Forces team and the Afghan Northern Alliance worked together. They surprised the Taliban in villages. Special Forces members radioed for bombers and fighter planes to attack Taliban camps. Others painted targets with lasers that guided the bombs. The Taliban fled the city within a few days. People greeted their American and Afghan liberators with joy.

Special Forces members must build relationships with local people.

Special Forces members must be strong and smart to complete their missions.

Special Forces are called "special" for a good reason. They are specially selected, specially trained, and specially equipped. Their missions support the U.S. Army and other military branches. Special Forces soldiers are used to extreme cold, hunger, and tiredness. They find creative solutions to thorny problems. Most of the soldiers are quiet but observant. All are committed to protecting and defending the United States and its allies.

AIR-STRIKE TECHNOLOGY

Special Forces "paint" targets with laser beams during air strikes. The battery-powered laser device weighs approximately 18 pounds (8 kg). It sits on a small tripod. The soldier looks through a telescope to line up the laser beam. Pilots flying overhead see the laser with special viewers. Pilots drop bombs on the lighted targets.

CHAPTER TWO: THE GROWTH OF ARMY SPECIAL FORCES

Successes in past wars helped shape the Special Forces over time. Rogers' Rangers fought in the French and Indian War (1754– 1763). They were a military unit of American frontiersmen. They struck their enemies with the speed and accuracy of a rattlesnake. Colonel John Mosby fought during the Civil War (1861–1865). His Confederate raiders destroyed Union supply trains. Mosby's men protected local people and won their trust. This skill is still used by Special Forces in modern times.

The Office of Strategic Services (OSS) handled intelligence and secret operations during World War II (1939–1945). Its members were mostly men but included a few women. OSS agents parachuted behind enemy lines. They trained and helped local people fighting the German and Japanese armies occupying their countries. After the war, President Harry S. Truman broke up the OSS. He did not want a secret police unit that could someday get out of control. But soon the Soviet Union threatened to invade Europe. So the new Central Intelligence Agency (CIA) took over the OSS intelligence operations. The new Army Special Forces took over warfare behind enemy lines.

President John F. Kennedy

THE GREEN BERET

In 1962, President John F. Kennedy called the Green Beret "a symbol of excellence, a badge of courage, a mark of distinction in the fight for freedom." Green Berets call themselves U.S. Army Special Forces, or just Special Forces.

Special Forces grew quickly in the 1960s. President John F. Kennedy realized the value of Special Forces for fighting U.S. enemies. Special Forces fought in the Vietnam War (1957–1975). They were part of the Salvadoran Civil War (1979–1992). They helped overthrow the dictator Manuel Noriega in Panama (1989). They played key roles in the Gulf War (1990–1991), Afghanistan (2001 to the present), and Iraq (2003–2010).

OPERATION KINGPIN

In May 1970, the United States was at war with North Vietnam. A U.S. pilot took photos over two North Vietnamese prisoner-of-war (POW) camps. The photos showed an American signal that meant, "Come and get us." Special Forces raided the camp on November 21, 1970, to rescue seventy U.S. POWs. Unfortunately, the prisoners were moved before the Special Forces arrived. The rescue failed, but the raid showed the North Vietnamese the U.S. Army would come for its men. The North Vietnamese put their American prisoners in a better camp. They treated the prisoners with more care. The Americans realized they had not been forgotten. They knew that one day they would be free. The prisoners regained their freedom in 1973.

Special Forces units have many jobs. They fight terrorists and conduct raids and ambushes. They perform reconnaissance. They help teach friendly foreign countries to defend themselves. They wage unconventional warfare against invaders in friendly countries.

Fighting Terrorism

Terrorists are the top enemy in the modern era. On September 11, 2001, the terrorist network al-Qaeda destroyed the World Trade Center in New York City and damaged the Pentagon near Washington, DC. Since that time, Army Special Forces have captured or killed many al-Qaeda members. Special Forces also train police in other countries to spot terrorist threats. The soldiers and police work together to keep terrorist groups from forming.

AL-QAEDA

Al-Qaeda issued a declaration of war against the United States in August 1996. Al-Qaeda works with other terrorist groups. Combined, they have killed thousands of civilians and soldiers around the world.

Sometimes Special Forces teams must get into and out of an area very quickly.

Conducting Raids and Ambushes

Special Forces teams perform quick raids and ambushes. They are often in and out before the enemy knows what happened. Sometimes teams rescue prisoners of war held in foreign countries. Sometimes Special Forces seize weapons or important information. Special Forces teams use quick strikes to break an enemy's hold on a country.

Performing Reconnaissance

Reconnaissance, or *recon,* means "looking around and gathering information without the enemy noticing." Special Forces teams gather information on enemy movements and weapons. The teams often work behind enemy lines. Special Forces soldiers in Afghanistan looked for enemy camps. They radioed in the camps' positions so U.S. planes could bomb them.

Special Forces members in Mali teach tactics to local soldiers.

Helping Foreign Countries Defend Themselves

Special Forces members teach soldiers of friendly nations to defend themselves. For instance, the illegal drug trade in several Latin American countries threatens peace and safety there. Special Forces teams train police and military forces to deal with violent drug dealers.

Sometimes Special Forces teams visit countries during peacetime. The teams teach the countries' soldiers to use equipment and weapons. The training helps these countries prepare for potential attacks. Special Forces try to form strong connections in these countries. The United States likes to have many allies to trade with. It works with these allies to improve world peace and stability.

"They're not supermen. They're just guys who won't quit."

—Larry, Special Forces team member

Waging Unconventional Warfare

Unconventional warfare is often called guerrilla warfare. Special Forces use this kind of warfare to liberate countries from enemy occupation. Teams usually enter the country secretly. They build friendships with the local people who are already fighting. Special Forces train these fighters to gather information about the enemy. They also train the fighters to do surprise attacks, such as blowing up enemy supply trucks and telephone lines. The goal is to free people from rulers they do not want. This is the motto of Army Special Forces: *De oppresso liber*, which is Latin for "Free the oppressed."

CHAPTER THREE: WARRIOR DIPLOMATS

Special Forces soldiers are some of the best warriors in the world. Many have had extensive schooling, and all receive special training. Yet they rarely go into a situation with guns blazing. A Special Forces team behind enemy lines is on its own. The team must deal with bad weather, lost gear, and disagreements with local people. The men would rather outsmart enemies than overpower them. A Special Forces team is called an Operational Detachment Alpha (ODA). It has twelve men. The team can split into two groups to cover a larger area if necessary.

Each ODA includes the following soldiers:

★ One commander. He is in charge during each mission.

★ One assistant commander. He backs up the commander. He leads a team if the ODA divides in two.

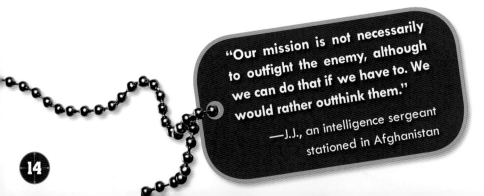

"Our mission is not necessarily to outfight the enemy, although we can do that if we have to. We would rather outthink them."

—J.J., an intelligence sergeant stationed in Afghanistan

Special Forces teams work together to carry heavy loads.

★ Two weapons sergeants. They operate and maintain a huge selection of weapons, such as machine guns, grenade launchers, and antitank missiles. They also act as snipers.

★ Two civil engineering sergeants. They construct buildings and bridges. They use explosives to blow up obstacles and enemy targets.

★ Two medical sergeants. They act as doctors, dentists, and veterinarians. They keep their teammates healthy. They also provide medical care to local people and their farm animals.

★ Two communications sergeants. They operate everything from the most modern satellite radios and computer systems to old-fashioned Morse code telegraphs.

★ One intelligence specialist. He gathers and studies important information about the enemy.

★ One operations sergeant. He helps the commander plan missions and train team members. He makes sure the team has the equipment it needs.

Army Special Forces are the most adaptive members of the U.S. military. Special Forces members must fit into many cultures around the world. They speak many languages. Teams work with people from many different races, backgrounds, and religions. Special Forces go wherever a threat exists to the United States or its allies. Special Forces went to Haiti in 1994. They helped stop a military dictator from taking over the government there.

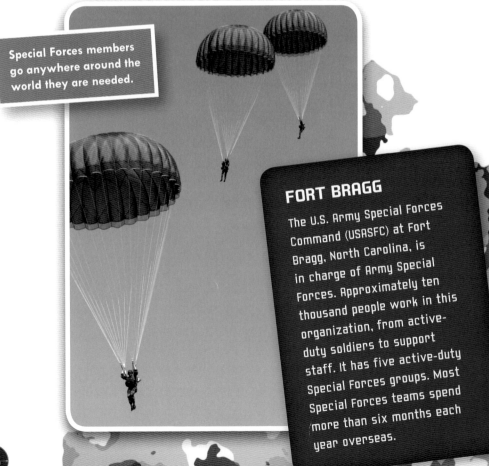

Special Forces members go anywhere around the world they are needed.

FORT BRAGG

The U.S. Army Special Forces Command (USASFC) at Fort Bragg, North Carolina, is in charge of Army Special Forces. Approximately ten thousand people work in this organization, from active-duty soldiers to support staff. It has five active-duty Special Forces groups. Most Special Forces teams spend more than six months each year overseas.

Haitians greeted Special Forces members in 1994.

On August 2, 1990, Iraq attacked Kuwait, a tiny desert country rich in oil. The United States and its allies pushed Iraq out of Kuwait in February 1991. After the war, many Special Forces teams trained Kuwaiti troops to fight if Iraq attacked again. One team taught how to use combat rifles. Another team trained snipers. Yet another taught how to radio in target coordinates to the Kuwaiti Air Force, which dropped practice bombs.

In 1999, Special Forces patrolled a city in Bosnia and Herzegovina when there was fighting among different ethnic groups. Special Forces drove unmarked vehicles and wore civilian clothes. They made friends with the local people. Special Forces helped track down war criminals. They worked to keep violence from starting again.

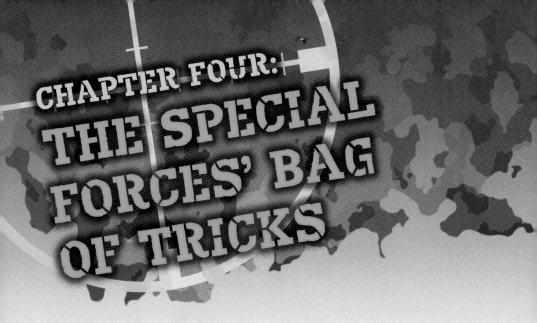

CHAPTER FOUR: THE SPECIAL FORCES' BAG OF TRICKS

Special Forces members are great planners. They have many decisions to make before each mission.

One of the first things Special Forces teams choose is their uniform. The soldiers have several choices depending on the land they plan to cover. Green, brown, beige, and black camouflage patterns are used for forest settings. Desert patterns come in three or six colors depending on the ground cover. City patterns include black, white, and gray for places with light-colored buildings. Shades of blue hide the team against dark buildings or in shadows. Cold weather requires heavy boots, pants, and parkas. Every Special Forces shirt or vest includes many pockets.

> "I will never surrender, though I be the last. If I am taken, I pray that I may have the strength to spit upon my enemy. My goal is to succeed in any mission—and to live to succeed again."
>
> —Special Forces Creed excerpt

Special Forces members must prepare for any weather.

Helmets and body armor protect them from bullets and pieces of metal from exploded bombs. The soldiers do not like to wear the hot and heavy gear, but they know their armor protects them.

Many Special Forces members say "going native" is the best camouflage in the world. Examples include turbans, tunics, and clothes made outside the United States.

Special Forces missions require specialized
gear, such as mountaineering equipment.

Each Special Forces mission determines the gear the team carries. A mission to help feed local people in a country at war requires large loads of food and medical supplies. These are often dropped by airplanes. Secret operations sometimes require Special Forces soldiers to carry everything on their backs.

Special Forces members often carry M4 rifles.

An ODA team usually arms itself with light, easy-to-carry personal weapons. The army-issued M4A1 carbine is a lightweight rifle. It also has add-ons, such as a grenade launcher, optical aiming sights, and night vision that allows soldiers to see in the dark. The M9 pistol is easy to carry in a holster or a pocket.

MISSION IN FOCUS
REBUILDING DIWANIYA

Special Forces arrived in the Iraqi city of Diwaniya in April 2003 after dictator Saddam Hussein was removed from power. The Americans were heroes, yet new problems happened every day. Rival tribes battled for control of the city. Stores remained closed. Government workers stayed home. The sewer treatment plant did not operate. Fuel supplies were low. Radios and televisions had no electricity.

Special Forces wanted the Iraqis to learn how to take charge of their city. "The Iraqis want us to . . . solve all their problems," the team leader said. "But I tell them: 'We are only twelve. You must start to do it yourselves.'"

The Special Forces braved the tribal violence. They used their communication skills to get the tribes talking to one another. Special Forces organized a local police force. Police recruits carried U.S. rifles and wore green armbands. Eventually, Diwaniya reopened for business.

Proper packing is essential on Special Forces missions.

Weight is very important if the soldiers have to lug equipment on their backs. Backpacks and belts help spread the weight across the soldier's shoulders and back. Containers and plastic ziplock bags protect their gear and keep it dry. When a Special Forces soldier parachutes out of a plane, he does not want his toothpaste to explode all over his GPS device!

The Special Forces soldiers are trained to endure hardships, but they have to eat sometimes. Some guys pack their favorite foods, such as beef jerky or candy. ODA teams inserted behind enemy lines cannot expect daily food supplies. Trash can be a problem on a secret mission. Sometimes the soldier carries it out in his gear. Other times he buries it where it won't be found and animals can't dig it up.

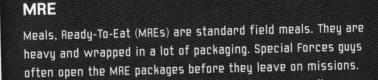

MRE

Meals, Ready-To-Eat (MREs) are standard field meals. They are heavy and wrapped in a lot of packaging. Special Forces guys often open the MRE packages before they leave on missions. They take out the food they like and repack it in smaller, lightweight plastic bags.

A soldier mixes together an MRE ration.

CHAPTER FIVE: THE PATH TO THE GREEN BERET

pecial Forces recruits must be males in excellent shape. Currently, the United States does not allow females to serve as ODA members.

Every Special Forces recruit already has military experience. Each soldier has also completed the U.S. Army Airborne School, where he learned to parachute out of an airplane. However, soldiers who wear the Green Beret require a lot more training.

First, recruits must pass the Special Forces Assessment and Selection (SFAS) course. SFAS involves twenty-four days of brutal testing. Out of

Special Forces training exercises simulate combat situations.

Special Forces members are the best of the best.

every one hundred recruits starting the test, an average of sixty-seven drop out. The course is never the same twice. Soldiers train in pouring rain or blistering heat. Every day begins with a brisk warm-up run. Then the real test of endurance begins. Recruits march or swim with 50-pound (23 kg) packs on their backs. They climb ropes and crawl through muddy underground pipes in obstacle courses. Later, they have to pinpoint targets for airstrikes. They must locate the targets with only a plastic protractor, a magnetic compass, and a paper map. No GPS allowed!

NO FEAR

Special Forces recruits who fear small spaces or tall heights fail the SFAS test. Marches and runs are designed to mentally and physically exhaust candidates. The tests discover if recruits will keep going no matter what.

Special Forces members must work as a team.

Sleep-deprived recruits have to solve challenging problems, such as crossing a river without getting wet. They have few tools and no boat. Team exercises test their ability to work together. For example, the team may have to move a jeep with a missing wheel using only poles and ropes. Recruits who argue with other team members fail SFAS.

The Qualification, or Q, Course is the next step for recruits who pass SFAS. The Q Course is divided into three parts. Part I is thirty-nine days long. Special Forces recruits practice field skills, such as navigating on land, conducting recon, and setting up ambushes. By the end of Part I, recruits can plan a mission, choose supplies, and lead a team cross-country with a full load of combat gear in any kind of weather.

During Part II, recruits receive specialty training for their job on an ODA. Classes include training in weapons, medicine, engineering, communications, and intelligence. Specialty training lasts for six months to one year. Part II also includes learning how to be a good teacher. Special Forces teams spend a lot of time teaching foreign soldiers.

Part III lasts thirty-eight days. Recruits spend more than half of this time on the final exam. The exam, called Operation Robin Sage, tests everything the recruits have learned. It is based on lessons learned by the OSS in World War II, when OSS soldiers behind enemy lines gained the trust of bands of local fighters.

Special Forces trainees must pass the Operation Robin Sage tests.

Graduates of Part III are awarded their Green Berets, but their training is not over. Each new Special Forces soldier learns at least one foreign language. Spanish, French, and German are often easier to learn. They only take a few months of schooling. Chinese, Arabic, and Russian may take more than a year.

After that, the recruits go to Survival, Evasion, Resistance, and Escape (SERE) School. SERE skills are secret, but each Special Forces soldier learns how to avoid capture, how to survive being in prison, and how to escape.

Next, every new Special Forces soldier attends advanced parachute training. Special Forces soldiers learn to jump out of airplanes flying very high. The higher the airplane flies, the more secret the team can be. Sometimes they open their chutes while they are still very high. This lets them glide quietly behind enemy lines. Other times they free-fall for two minutes to get close to the ground. They hurtle through the air at 125 miles (200 kilometers) per hour before popping open their chute and landing silently.

Special Forces members proudly wear the Green Beret.

Special Forces members must practice their parachuting skills.

"How you know we're doing our job right is when you don't know we're there. We'll never fire a shot; not even the dogs bark."

—Anonymous Special Forces soldier

The Special Forces have no ideal type of soldier. Each soldier's strength comes from his skills and his knowledge. The last line of the Special Forces Creed says, "I am a member of my nation's chosen soldiery. God grant that I may not be found wanting, that I will not fail this sacred trust. De oppresso liber (Free the oppressed)."

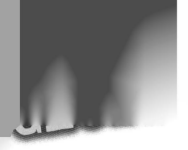

ALLIES
friendly nations that often help one another in wars

AL-QAEDA
violent terrorist organization responsible for the September 11, 2001, attacks in the United States

AMBUSH
surprise attack from a hidden position

CHOPPER
slang term for helicopter

CIVILIAN
person not serving in the military

DIPLOMAT
person who helps resolve conflict without violence

INTELLIGENCE
information of military or political value

ODA
Operational Detachment Alpha; a twelve-man team of Special Forces soldiers

OPPRESSED
people forced to submit to a brutal government

RECON
reconnaissance, or secret information gathering

TALIBAN
militant Islamic movement of Pashtun tribesmen from around Afghanistan

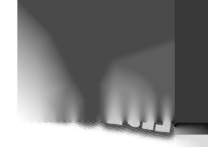

Further Reading

Hamilton, John. *Green Berets*. Minneapolis: Abdo, 2012.

Labrecque, Ellen. *Heroic Jobs: Special Forces*. Chicago: Raintree, 2012.

Lusted, Marcia Amidon. *Air Commandos*. Minneapolis: Lerner Publications, 2014.

Sutherland, Adam. *Special Forces*. Minneapolis: Lerner Publications, 2011.

Websites

Army Special Forces: Green Berets

http://www.baseops.net/militarybooks/greenberets.html

This website includes a brief summary of Special Forces history, selection, and missions. Be sure to watch the Fox News video of Special Forces up close in Afghanistan.

How the Green Berets Work

http://science.howstuffworks.com/green-beret1.htm

This website includes easy-to-read facts, maps, and videos.

United States Army Special Operations Command

http://www.soc.mil

This website is the online home of all Army Special Operations, including Army Rangers, the John F. Kennedy Special Warfare Center and School, Special Forces, and Psychological Operations.

Afghanistan, 4–6, 9, 11

al-Qaeda, 10

ambushes, 10–11, 27

armor, 19

Central Intelligence Agency, 8

creed, 18, 29

equipment, 12, 16, 22

Fort Bragg, 16

Green Berets, 9, 24, 28

helicopters, 4

intelligence, 8, 16, 27

Iraq, 9, 17, 21

Kennedy, John F., 9

languages, 5, 16, 28

lasers, 6, 7

Mosby, John, 8

motto, 13

MRE, 23

Office of Strategic Services, 8, 27

Operational Detachment Alpha, 14–16, 21, 23, 24, 27

Operation Enduring Freedom, 4

Operation Kingpin, 10

Operation Robin Sage, 27

packs, 4, 22, 25

parachuting, 6, 8, 22, 24, 28

Qualification Course, 26–27

reconnaissance, 10, 11, 27

Rogers' Rangers, 8

Special Forces Assessment and Selection, 24–26

Survival, Evasion, Resistance, and Escape School, 28

Taliban, 4–5, 6

teaching, 10, 12, 13, 17, 27

teamwork, 14–16, 26

terrorism, 10

training, 5, 7, 14, 23, 24–28

Truman, Harry S., 8

unconventional warfare, 10, 13

uniforms, 18–19

Vietnam War, 9, 10

weapons, 11, 12, 15, 21, 27

About the Author

Patricia Newman is the author of several books for children, including *Jingle the Brass*, a Junior Library Guild Selection and a Smithsonian-recommended book; and *Nugget on the Flight Deck*, a California Reading Association Eureka! Silver Honor Book for Nonfiction. Watch for *Plastic, Ahoy!* from Millbrook Press in 2014. Visit her at www.patriciamnewman.com.